BARBS FROM THE
BARD

BARBS FROM THE BARD

Shakespearean Insults

with modern translations and notes

Michael Viner
Stefan Rudnicki

NEW MILLENNIUM PRESS

Beverly Hills

Library of Congress Cataloging-in-Publication Data

Shakespeare, William, 1564–1616.
    Barbs from the bard : Shakespearean insults with modern translations and notes / [compiled by] Michael Viner, Stefan Rudnicki ; foreword by Roger Rees.
      p. cm.
    ISBN 1-893224-20-1
    1. Shakespeare, William, 1564–1616—Quotations. 2. Invective—Quotations, maxims, etc. 3. Quotations, English. I. Viner, Michael. II. Rudnicki, Stefan, 1945– III. Title.

    Pr2892.V56 2000
    822.3'3--dc21

00-028355

Printed in the United States of America

New Millennium Press
a division of NM WorldMedia, Inc.
350 S. Beverly Drive
Suite 315
Beverly Hills, California 90212
www.newmillenniumpress.com

10 9 8 7 6 5 4 3 2 1

Contents

Foreword

As the new millennium begins, amid the accelerating excitement of progress, I feel something is missing. Something of mine is being eroded away—my individuality—and I want to do something to get it back. We Little People—I assume you're about my size—we're being lost in the technological poker game, and it makes me so mad that I almost want to say a naughty word! Eventually, they say, the races of the world will intermingle, and every skin will be beige. I just worry that our minds will finish up beige, too.

Perceptively, the powers-that-be are controlling everything we do. Who the powers-that-be are I have no idea, but I feel I can be pretty certain that they know who *I* am. They've got *my* number, for sure. They know the car I drive, the color, number of dents on the fender—the lot. My medical history? Sure, they've seen it, and they'll sell it to any quack who passes through their office. And never a word to me until I'm solicited by mail to participate in a sweat-lodged, Tupperware weekend for two in Utah at three hundred dollars a sweat—gratuities not included, parking extra.

It makes me want to say a naughty word! It makes me mad! They stuff the little postcards in every magazine I buy; they mail the catalogues by the hundreds every day, and e-mail by the dumpster on the hour, every hour. Doesn't this invasion of your privacy make *you* mad? Don't you want to fight back, complain and yell about the dreadful traffic, the nutty government, the deadly pollution, and, even worse, the guy who stole my parking spot in Pasadena yesterday? Don't you want to shout out about the whole mess, the absolute unfairness of it all?

My parents can remember a sweeter, gentler time, when, at the corner shop, you'd present a list to the grocer and he'd offer you a seat, which you'd take while *he* ran to collect the requested comestibles.

Something must be done, Little People. I'd run up to the powers-that-be and scream, "Sh—," or perhaps even the dreaded "F" word. But why bother? Familiarity breeds familiarity, and nowadays the strength of the Anglo-Saxon expletive is sadly diluted. Random usage has weakened them to the point that we'll soon be hearing them on *Sesame Street*.

But help is at hand! Don't get mad, as they say; get even. Despair not! Run into that supermarket, walk up to that manager, and ask him to try this on for size: "You leathern jerken, crystal-button, knotty-pated, agate-ring, puke-stocking, caddis-garter, smooth-tongue, Spanish pouch!" And see what he says, adding as you leave, perhaps, "Mome, malthorse, capon, coxcomb, idiot, patch!" And, as a parting shot, "Fat paunches have lean pates."

Phone that irritating magazine publisher or e-mail him this piece of your mind: "Boils and plagues plaster you o'er, that you may be abhorr'd farther than seen, and one infect another against the wind a mile." Feel better? Of course you do!

Here is one book you can't put down because it's so cathartic—*Barbs from the Bard*. Insult *me* in the future, and you'll hear no worn-out "d—n" cross my lips. You'll get an "Odds bodikins!" and a command to "Make thy sepulchre, and creep into it far before thy time!"

At last, we are empowered, Little People, Romans, countrymen. There *is* a way of fighting back. You're reading it right now. Sweet vengeance is just around the corner. I swear!

ROGER REES
JANUARY 2000

INTRODUCTION

Shakespeare, for most of us, is our earliest touchstone to humor in great literature. In the history of mankind no one—from the classical Greek playwrights to Neil Simon—has written as many plays that have combined all the elements and that have lasted and will last throughout recorded time.

There is no deeper well of recorded humor than the works of the Bard of Avon. Even today much of our humor is based on Shakespeare's plays—from the Academy Award-winning film *Shakespeare in Love* to the myriad of remake movies that we see time and time again. Everyone tries to update the plays of the Bard; few manage to do it successfully.

There seem to be an infinite number of jokes about Shakespeare and the difficulty of properly acting the various roles in his plays, especially in America. One of the classic stories involves a well-known but not talented actress who was playing the role of Ophelia in

Hamlet at one of New York's Shakespeare in the Park festivals. The audience was not responding in any positive way to her performance and as time went on they started throwing tomatoes and other fruit at her. Finally the young lady could take it no longer. She stepped to the front of the stage and said, "Listen, I'm just an actress, I didn't write this crap."

In today's world, where the put-down is often a lost art and many times is relegated to just a hand gesture or some other crass verbal comment, Shakespeare's verbiage stands out as a beacon to us all of how wit and humor can be combined to make a point and give not only a retort but a laugh as well. This book gives the option and the opportunity to widen our vocabulary and our minds and learn the art of the truly eloquent put-down and the art and precision of the English language.

It is our hope that this small tome may serve as a gentle reminder and inspiration that the pen is not only mightier than the sword but is also a lot sharper and a lot funnier.

I hope you have as much enjoyment reading this book as we had plagiarizing the greatest playwright in history.

MICHAEL VINER

BARBS FROM THE BARD

THE GOOD

To be used against those that are too
good to be true, or whose goodness
stands in the way of seduction

Your virginity breeds mites, much like a cheese.
All's Well That Ends Well I, I

Translation: Let's make it before you start to gather moss.

He hath bought a pair of cast lips of Diana. A nun
of winter's sisterhood kisses not more religiously,
the very ice of chastity is in them.

As You Like It III, 4

Translation: What a cold fish!

(Diana is the Roman goddess of chastity, also personified in
the cold moon. In this case any conceivable warmth of contact
is even more removed by suggesting that the lips in question
are merely a copy of the original and bought for cash.)

She's able to freeze the god Priapus, and
undo a whole generation.

Pericles IV, 6

Translation: She's a real turn-off.

(Priapus, the son of Dionysus and Aphrodite, was regarded by
the Greeks as a god of fruitfulness, and was represented in
carved images in the form of a phallus. It is suggested here that
the virtuous Marina, to whom this refers, could prevent
the birth of an entire generation of children.)

Thou wilt fall backward when thou hast more wit.

Romeo and Juliet I, 3

Translation: You'll get what's coming to you when the
time comes. And you'll love it.

(The Nurse chides Juliet by suggesting that she is still
too young to appreciate sex.)

He thinks too much. Such men are dangerous.

Julius Caesar I, 2

Translation: Watch your shirt!
or
Still waters run deep.

(The appearance of virtue, in the form of thoughtfulness
and contemplation, hides malice.)

The lunatic, the lover, and the poet
Are of imagination all compact.

A Midsummer Night's Dream V, 1

Translation: You're all nuts!

(All three are made up of nothing but imaginings. This is either
the most dismissive insult or the greatest compliment.)

THE BAD

---•⚬•---

To be used to identify evil,
and then to disarm it

Your villainy goes against my weak stomach,
and therefore I must cast it up.

Henry V III, 2

Translation: You make me sick.

O, if men were to be saved by merit, what hole in hell were
hot enough for you?

Henry IV Part 1: I, 2

Translation: You're the lowest of the low, by any
standard worth naming.

One may smile, and smile, and be a villain.

Hamlet I, 5

Translation: Shining face, soul of pitch.

Assume a virtue, if you have it not.

Hamlet III, 4

Translation: At least pretend you've got some shame.

Thy sin's not accidental, but a trade.

Measure for Measure III, 1

Translation: You're a real pro . . .

Thou art unfit for any place but hell.

Richard III I, 2

Translation: Go where you belong.

All goodness is poison to thy stomach.

Henry VIII III, 2

Translation: You live on evil.

Thy food is such as has been belch'd on by infected lungs.

Pericles IV, 6

Translation: You are nourished by disease.

Think him as a serpent's egg, which, hatch'd,
would, as his kind, grow mischievous.

Julius Caesar II, I

Translation: He's a disaster waiting to happen.

You are like an envious sneaping frost
That bites the first-born infants of the spring.

Love's Labours Lost I, I

Translation: Out of jealousy, you'll squeeze the life and
hope out of anything that shows promise.

(To *sneap* means to pinch or nip.)

More validity, more honorable state, more
courtship lives in carrion flies.

Romeo and Juliet III, 3

Translation: You have less worth, dignity, and
manners than a maggot.

Frailty, thy name is woman.

Hamlet I, 2

Translation: Earth girls are easy.

'Tis beauty that doth oft makes women proud,
But God he knows thy share thereof is small.
'Tis virtue that doth make them most admir'd,
The contrary doth make thee wonder'd at.
'Tis government that makes them seem divine,
The want thereof makes thee abominable.
Thou art as opposite to every good
As the Antipodes are unto us.

Henry VI, Part 3: I, 4

Translation: You're ugly, sinful, out of control; the flip side
of everything that's decent.

(*Antipodes* are people who live on the opposite side of the globe.)

O tiger's heart wrapp'd in a woman's hide!

Henry VI, Part 3: I, 4

Translation: Dragon Lady!

O most insatiate and luxurious woman!
Titus Andronicus V, 1

Translation: Nympho!

Thou art the pandar to her dishonor.
Cymbeline III, 4

Translation: Pimp!

I knew him to be a dangerous and lascivious boy, who is a
whale to virginity, and devours up all the fry it finds.
All's Well That Ends Well IV, 3

Translation: Little girls are meat to him.
He wolfs 'em all down.

You are polluted with your lusts,
Stain'd with the guiltless blood of innocents,
Corrupt and tainted with a thousand vices.

Henry VI, Part 1: V, 4

Translation: You are one bad dude.

He professes not keeping of oaths. In breaking
'em he is stronger than Hercules.

All's Well That Ends Well IV, 3

Translation: He's a powerful profaner of promises.

His vows . . . are brokers
Breathing like sanctified and pious bawds
The better to beguile.

Hamlet I, 3

Translation: He's a hypocrite, a silver-tongued devil.

You'll surely sup in hell.

Henry VI Part 2: V, 1

Translation: You've got till dark. Then it's over for you.

THE UGLY

Exorcisms of the unlovely,
in appearance, spirit, or deed

Go get thee hence,
Hadst thou Narcissus in thy face, to me
Thou wouldst appear most ugly.

Antony and Cleopatra II, 5

Translation: No matter how attractive others
find you, to me you're gross.

(In classical mythology, Narcissus was known for his
extreme beauty. Upon seeing his reflection in a fountain,
he became so infatuated with his own face that he could
not bear to look away. There he starved until he was
transformed into the flower that bears his name.)

Where wilt thou find a cavern dark enough
to mask thy monstrous visage?

Julius Caesar II, 1

Translation: The best you can do is try to hide.

(The suggestion here is that true ugliness will remain visible, shine
even, until there is not the smallest glimmer of light to see it by.)

The tartness of his face sours ripe grapes.

Coriolanus V, 4

Translation: Sourpuss!

Do you amend thy face, and I'll amend my life.

Henry IV Part I: III, 3

Translation: Mind your own business, ugly!

His complexion is perfect gallows.

The Tempest I, 1

Translation: He is pale as death.

Whatsoever cunning fiend it was
That wrought upon thee so preposterously
Hath got the voice in hell for excellence.

Henry V II, 2

Translation: Whoever got you looking like that
took the monster prize.

Your hair hangs like flax on a distaff,
and I hope to see a housewife take thee
between her legs, and spin it off.

Twelfth Night I, 3

Translation: A roll in the hay might help.

(A *distaff* is a tool for spinning wool or flax into thread. It is also
a word for a woman or the female sex in general. Thus Sir
Andrew Aguecheek, the butt of this insult, is not only having a
bad hair day, he is also considered effeminate.)

I will beat thee into handsomeness!

Troilus and Cressida II, 1

Translation: It couldn't hurt.

Sell when you can, you are not for all markets.

As You Like It III, 5

Translation: Take what (whom) you can get,
and consider yourself lucky.

Heap of wrath, foul indigested lump,
As crooked in thy manners as thy shape!

Henry VI Part 2: V, 1

Thou art neither like thy sire nor dam,
But like a foul misshapen stigmatic,
Mark'd by the Destinies to be avoided,
As venom toads, or lizards' dreadful stings.

Henry VI Part 3: II, 2

Thy mother felt more than a mother's pain,
And yet brought forth less than a mother's hope.

Henry VI Part 3: V, 6

Teeth hadst thou in thy head when thou wast born,
To signify thou cam'st to bite the world.

Henry VI Part 3: V, 6

Out of my sight! Thou dost infect my eyes.

Richard III I, 2

Translation: You are the most hideous creature ever
imagined, and your morally and physically deformed
existence is an insult to your parents and a
dangerous blot upon the world.

(The above summarizes the previous five quotes, which all refer to
Richard of Gloucester, who later became Richard III. Shakespeare
made him the epitome of everything repulsive and grotesque.)

The Boring

(AND OTHERWISE VERBALLY DISADVANTAGED)

To be used in an effort to render
others speechless

More of your conversation would infect my brain.

Coriolanus II, 1

Translation: Shut up!

More matter with less art.

Hamlet II, 2

Translation: Get to the point.

The music of his own vain tongue
Doth ravish him like enchanting harmony.

Love's Labours Lost I, 1

Translation: He loves to hear himself talk.

What cracker is this same that deafs our ears
With this abundance of superfluous breath?

King John II, 1

Translation: What a windbag!

(A *cracker* is one who boasts.)

Well said! That was laid on with a trowel.

As You Like It I, 2

Translation: Slicing it thick, aren't we?

Sweet smoke of rhetoric!

Love's Labours Lost III, 1

Translation: Nothing but a smokescreen!

I wonder that you will still be talking.
Nobody marks you.

Much Ado About Nothing I, 1

Translation: Why go on? No one's listening.

Dost dialogue with thy shadow?

Timon of Athens II, 2

Translation: Who are you talking to?

How quaint an orator you are.

Henry VI Part 2: III, 2

Translation: Daintily said.

Have I lived to stand at the taunt
of one who makes fritters of English?

The Merry Wives of Windsor V, 5

Translation: He dares to insult me?
The best he can do is fry the language!

(The reference is to foreigners—in this case, a Welshman—who
try to use the language without properly understanding it.)

His speech was like a tangled chain, nothing
impaired, but all disordered.

A Midsummer Night's Dream V, 1

Translation: Can't make heads or tails of what he said.

He hath never fed of the dainties that are bred in a book.
He hath not eat paper, as it were. He hath not drunk ink.
His intellect is not replenished.

Love's Labours Lost IV, 2

Translation: He's illiterate, and so lacks experience
of the finest life has to offer.

They have been at the great feast of languages,
and stolen the scraps.

Love's Labours Lost V, 1

Translation: A crumb mistaken for the loaf.

You unlettered small-knowing soul.

Love's Labours Lost I, 1

Translation: Moron!

Thou wast not wont to be so dull.

Richard III IV, 2

Translation: You used to be sharper.

There will little learning die then that day thou art hang'd.

Timon of Athens II, 2

Translation: The world won't miss your wit
and wisdom when you die.

If you spend word for word with me,
I shall make your wit bankrupt.

Two Gentlemen of Verona II, 4

Translation: Try to trade insults with me
and you're doomed.

Repair thy wit, good youth, or it will fall
To cureless ruin.

The Merchant of Venice IV, 1

Translation: Use your head, kid, before it's too late.

THE LARGE

Comments to deflate the overblown

Fat paunches have lean pates.

Love's Labours Lost I, 1

Translation: The fatter you are,
the dumber you get.

You show yourself highly fed and lowly taught.

All's Well That Ends Well II, 2

Translation: You are fat and stupid.

Feed, and be fat.

Henry IV Part 2: II, 4

Translation: Eat up, fatso!

Leave gormandizing. The grave doth gape
For thee thrice wider than for other man.

Henry IV Part 2: V, 5

Translation: Stop eating. You're already 3X.

There's no room for faith, truth,
nor honesty in this bosom of thine.
It is all filled up with guts and midriff.

Henry IV Part 1: III, 3

Translation: You're so fat there's no space
left for anything else.

He sweats to death,
and lards the lean earth as he walks along.

Henry IV Part I: II, 2

Translation: His excretions fertilize the land.

Then did the sun on dunghill shine.

The Merry Wives of Windsor I, 3

Translation: Reeking to high heaven.

She's the kitchen wench, and all grease, and
I know not what use to put her to but to make a lamp
of her, and run from her by her own light.

In what part of her body stands Ireland?
Marry, sir, in her buttocks. I found it out by the bogs.

Where Spain?
Faith, I saw it not. But I felt it hot in her breath.

Where stood Belgia, the Netherlands?
O, sir, I did not look so low.

The Comedy of Errors III, 2

Translation: She's really huge.

(This geography lesson doubles as gross sophomoric anatomical
humor and good-natured fun at the expense of Britain's neigh-
bors. The damp bogs and fens of Ireland—note that in English
slang a *bog* is also an outhouse or privy—are contrasted with
Spain's heat and the Lowlands' position at or below sea level.)

THE SMALL, THE STUPID

(AND OTHERWISE INSIGNIFICANT)

*Pronouncements to abrogate
the unworthy*

So, my good window of lattice, fare thee well;
thy casement I need not open, for I look through thee.

All's Well That Ends Well II, 3

Translation: You're transparent.

or

I can see right through you.

(The image here is of a window equipped with a hinged
casement or sash. But because the covering is lattice,
composed of crossed strips that let in light, there
is no need to open the casement to see.)

You are not worth another word,
else I'd call you knave.

All's Well That Ends Well II, 3

Translation: I'd as soon insult you as talk to you.

You breathe in vain.
Timon of Athens III, 5

Translation: You're wasting your time.

Were I like thee I'd throw away myself.
Timon of Athens IV, 3

Translation: If I were you, I'd kill myself.

She is too mean to have her name repeated.

All's Well That Ends Well III, 5

Translation: She's not worth the time of day.

I should be angry with you if the time were convenient.

Henry V IV, I

Translation: I have no energy to waste on you.

I took thee for thy better.

Hamlet III, 4

Translation: I thought you were someone worth dealing with. My mistake.

What a disgrace is it to me to remember thy name?

Henry IV Part 2: II, 2

Translation: I recognized you. Shame on me.

Thou little better thing than earth!

Richard II III, 4

Translation: Clod!

You are not worth the dust
which the rude wind blows in your face.

King Lear IV, 2

Translation: Gone with the wind.

You three-inch fool.
The Taming of the Shrew IV, 1

Translation: Get Shorty.

You starveling, you eel-skin, you dried neat's-tongue,
you bull's pizzle, you stock-fish—
O for breath to utter what is like thee!—
you tailor's-yard, you sheath, you bow-case,
you vile standing tuck!

Henry IV Part 1: II, 4

Translation: You puny, scrawny, flimsy nothing!

(Upon being reminded of his girth by his companion Prince Hal,
the fat Falstaff counters by attacking the prince's slimness. A
starveling is one who is dying of starvation. A *neat* is an ox.
A *tuck* is a rapier. The other references should be obvious.)

Thou drone, thou snail, thou slug, thou sot.

The Comedy of Errors II, 2

Translation: You parasitic, lazy, slimy drunk!

(Alternately, *drone* can mean the monotonous,
low tone produced by an organ.)

You are one that converses more with the buttock of the
night than with the forehead of the morning.

Coriolanus II, 1

Translation: Your brains are in your ass.

You are a man made after supper of a cheese-paring.

Henry IV Part 2: III, 2

Translation: You're a smelly leftover.

Small curs are not regarded when they grin.

Henry VI Part 2: III, 1

Translation: Buzz off, puppy face.

I do wish thou wert a dog,
That I might love thee something.

Timon of Athens IV, 3

Translation: You're less than a son of a bitch.

Does not the stone rebuke you
For being more stone than it?

The Winter's Tale V, 3

Translation: Are you the quiet type,
or are you just dead?

You are weaker than a woman's tear,
Tamer than sleep, fonder than ignorance,
Less valiant than the virgin in the night,
And skilless as unpractis'd infancy.

Troilus and Cressida I, 1

Translation: Babe in the woods.
Ninety-pound weakling.

To die by thee were but to die in jest.

Henry VI Part 2: III, 2

Translation: Hit me! Go ahead, hit me!

You are a slight unmeritable man,
meet to be sent on errands.

Juliuꝛ Caeꝛar IV, I

Translation: You're not running for office.
You're running for coffee.

Though we lay these honors on this man,
he shall but bear them as the ass bears gold.

Juliuꝛ Caeꝛar IV, I

Translation: He's a four-star schmuck!

Now does he feel his title
Hang loose about him, like a giant's robe
Upon a dwarfish thief.

Macbeth V, 2

Translation: He's too small for his britches.

He is a proper man's picture, but alas!
who can converse with a dumb-show?

The Merchant of Venice I, 2

Translation: You can dress him up,
but you can't take him anywhere.

He shall die a flea's death.

The Merry Wives of Windsor IV, 2

Translation: He'll be a nothing right up to the end.

Get you gone, you dwarf,
You minimus, of hindering knot-grass made,
You bead, you acorn.

A Midsummer Night's Dream III, 2

Translation: Split, nebbish!

(A *minimus* is a tiny or insignificant creature;
also the smallest toe or finger.
Knot-grass is characterized by nodes or
bumps in the stems; hence *hindering*.)

Let him that moved you hither
Remove you hence. I knew at the first
You were a movable.

The Taming of the Shrew II, 1

Translation: Hey! Whoever left this accessory
here, take it away!

or

Garbage in, garbage out.

(A *movable* can be a personal possession or a piece of furniture, in
either case something with no real, or landed, value. In her next
line, Kate, when asked what she means by *movable*, calls
Petruchio a *joint-stool*.)

Her beauty and her brain go not together.

Cymbeline I, 3

Translation: Valley girl!

Any man may sing her, if he can take her clef.
She's noted.

Troilus and Cressida V, 2

Translation: She's been around the park.

(*Clef* means key, both musical and otherwise. *Noted*
is a pun denoting that she has been played before,
and is noted, or infamous, for it.)

Thou anatomy, thou!

Henry IV Part 2: V, 4

Translation: You speck!

THE MANY

To be used to disperse mobs and gangs

You common cry of curs! whose breath I hate
As reek o' th' rotten fens, whose loves I prize
As the dead carcasses of unburied men
That do corrupt my air.

Coriolanus III, 3

Translation: I hate crowds.

I have seen better faces in my time
Than stands on any shoulder that I see
Before me at this instant.

King Lear II, 2

Translation: You're the scruffiest-looking crew
I've ever seen.

You blocks, you stones, you worse than senseless things!

Julius Caesar I, 1

Translation: Together, your I.Q. doesn't add up to 73.

You caterpillars of the commonwealth!

Richard II II, 3

Translation: Parasites!

You are noisome weeds which without profit suck
The soil's fertility from wholesome flowers.

Richard II III, 4

Translation: Bloodsuckers!

(*Noisome* means offensive or noxious.)

Let no assembly of twenty be without a score of villains.

Timon of Athens III, 6

Translation: Rotten, to a man.

or

You're batting a thousand in the creep league.

(A *score* is twenty.)

For these my present friends, as they are to me nothing, so in nothing bless them, and to nothing are they welcome.

Timon of Athens III, 6

Translation: They're no pals of mine.

Live loath'd, and long,
Most smiling, smooth, detested parasites,
Courteous destroyers, affable wolves, meek bears,
You fools of fortune, trencher-friends, time's flies,
Cap-and-knee slaves, vapors, and minute-jacks!

Timon of Athens III, 6

Translation: Wusses. Obsequious sycophants,
toadies, fickle flatterers, parasites.

(A *trencher* is a plate; so a *trencher-friend* is a parasite. *Cap-and-knee* probably refers to the habit of taking of one's hat and kneeling in deference to authority. Vapors are exhalations or breaths. A *minute-jack* is a fickle person, one who changes his mind every minute. The passage suggests that their worst punishment would be to live long and so have to put up with themselves, each other, and the contempt of the world at large.)

Breath infect breath,
That their society, as their friendship, may
Be merely poison.

Timon of Athens IV, 1

Translation: Hang together, homes.
or
They deserve each other.

Was ever feather so lightly blown to and
fro as this multitude?

Henry VI *Part 2: IV, 8*

Translation: Want to be flavor of the week . . . today?

Oh, were my eyeballs into bullets turn'd,
That I in rage might shoot them at your faces!

Henry VI *Part 1: IV, 7*

Translation: If only looks could kill.

The Cowardly

To chase away the fearful

Taste your legs, sir, put them to motion.
Twelfth Night III, 1

Translation: Run away!

Take a good heart, and counterfeit to be a man.
As You Like It IV, 3

Translation: At least show the pretense of courage.

I will kill thee a hundred and fifty ways.
Therefore tremble and depart.
As You Like It V, 1

Translation: Split or be halved.

You cowards, you were got in fear.

Coriolanus I, 3

Translation: Your heritage is cowardice.

He never broke any man's head but his own,
and that was against a post when he was drunk.

Henry V III, 2

Translation: His only acts of daring were against himself.

You are the hare of whom the proverb goes,
Whose valor plucks dead lions by the beard.

King John II, 1

Translation: You can beat anyone, with both hands
tied behind *his* back.

You should be women,
And yet your beards forbid me to interpret
That you are so.

Macbeth I, 3

Translation: Sissies!

Thou wilt be as valiant as the wrathful dove,
or most magnanimous mouse.

Henry IV Part 2: III, 2

Translation: Five foot two, who's scared of you?

THE POORLY DRESSED

(AND OTHERWISE OVER- OR UNDERDECORATED)

*Fashion statements for
the unfashionable*

You have an undressed, unpolished, uneducated, unpruned,
untrained, or rather unlettered,
or ratherest, unconfirmed fashion.

Love's Labours Lost IV, 2

Translation: What *are* you wearing?
or
What were you thinking?
or
The emperor's new clothes?

He came ever in the rearward of fashion.

Henry IV Part 2: III, 2

Translation: Once a bum, always a bum.

The scarfs and the bannerets about thee did
manifoldly dissuade me from believing thee a vessel
of too great a burden.

All's Well That Ends Well II, 3

Translation: If the clothes make the man,
I was unimpressed.
or
A definite lightweight.

(The image is nautical, and suggests a ship decked
out in full regalia.)

There can be no kernel in this light nut.
The soul of this man is in his clothes.

All's Well That Ends Well II, 5

Translation: All icing, no cake!

Seems he a dove? His feathers are but borrow'd.

Henry VI Part 2: III, 1

Translation: He is not what he appears.

She's rustling in unpaid-for silk.

Cymbeline III, 3

Translation: She's living beyond her means.

God hath given you one face and
you make yourselves another.

Hamlet III, 1

Translation: You're vain and unnatural.

A tailor made thee.

King Lear II, 2

Translation: You are without substance.

A monster, a very monster in apparel.

The Taming of the Shrew III, 2

Translation: A freak of fashion.

(To be a monster was to be unnatural.)

THE MARRIED

Reflections and expostulations about
avoidance and regret

What should I do with a husband?
Dress him in my apparel and make him
my waiting-gentlewoman?

Much Ado About Nothing II, 1

Translation: I have no use for a domesticated man.

I would not marry her, though she were endowed with all
that Adam had left him before he transgressed.

Much Ado About Nothing II, 1

Translation: Not even if it's all about Eve.

Thinkest thou, though her father be very rich,
any man is so very a fool to be married to hell?

The Taming of the Shrew I, 1

Translation: Is any amount of money worth putting up
with that she-devil?

Woo her, wed her, and bed her,
and rid the house of her.

The Taming of the Shrew I, 1

Translation: Take my daughter . . . please.

To marry him is hopeless,
To be his whore is witless.

The Two Noble Kinsmen II, 4

Translation: Between a rock and a hard place.

O curse of marriage,
That we can call these delicate creatures ours,
And not their appetites! I had rather be a toad,
And live upon the vapor in a dungeon,
Than keep a corner in a thing I love,
For others' uses.

Othello III, 3

Translation: All or nothing.

Your wife is slippery.
The Winter's Tale I, 2

Translation: She gets around.

Till I have no wife I have nothing.
All's Well That Ends Well III, 2

Translation: Freedom, now!

GENERAL ABUSE

---— ❧ —---

Used for name calling
(an exercise in building a vocabulary
that few will understand, allowing
you to insult with impunity)

Mome, malthorse, capon, coxcomb, idiot, patch!
Comedy of Errors III, 1

Translation: Dolt, beast, chicken, eunuch, fool, clown.

(A *mome* is a blockhead. A *malthorse* is a heavy, laboring animal used by brewers. A *capon* is a castrated cock, and so resonates with ideas like emasculation and cowardice. A *coxcomb* is the hat worn by a fool or jester, and, by extension, a fool. A *patch* is a paltry fellow or clown.)

Doth thy other mouth call me?
The Tempest II, 2

Translation: Are you farting at me?

You witch, you hag, you baggage, you polecat, you ronyon!

The Merry Wives of Windsor IV, 2

Translation: Crone, shrew; superfluous, mangy skunk.

(*Baggage* is a term of contempt for a worthless woman. The
polecat of Shakespeare's experience is a skunklike mammal, that
also exudes a strong scent. A *ronyon* is a mangy creature.)

You scullion! You rampallian! You fustilarian!
I'll tickle your catastrophe!

Henry IV Part 2: II, 1

Translation: Idiotic tramp! I'm on your tail.

(Except for *scullion*, which is a term for the most menial
servant, the words in this attack are invented. *Rampallian*
seems to be a female ruffian, while *fustilarian* is a term of
reproach possibly associated with the word *fustian*, which
means high-sounding but nonsensical. *Catastrophe*, a dramatic
term referring to the conclusion, denouement, or climax
of play, here refers to a woman's backside.)

You leathern-jerkin, crystal-button, knotty-pated,
agate-ring, puke-stocking, caddis-garter,
smooth-tongue, Spanish pouch!

Henry IV Part I: II, 4

Translation: You overblown, paltry,
insinuating bag of wind.

(Most of these terms apply to articles of clothing and furnishings.
The quote begins by describing the object of the tirade—an
innkeeper—then little by little diminishing his status. So, while
leathern-jerkin and *crystal-button* seem to have little negative
connotation, *knotty-pated* means blockheaded, and *agate-ring*
is a diminutive referring to miniature carvings that were
common on such rings. While *puke-stocking* refers to a dark
color of hose, the word *puke* has obvious associations. Also,
a *caddis-garter* would have been made of a kind of worsted tape
or binding that was considered unfashionable. A *smooth-tongue*
could refer to mild or gentle speech, but also suggests the
insinuating talk of a malicious gossip. Finally, a *Spanish pouch*
is an insult to the innkeeper's wine, but also brings to
mind possibilities of venereal disease.)

O thou thing!

The Winter's Tale II, 1

Translation: You're it!

———————————— ❧ ————————————

Thou disease of a friend!

Timon of Athens III, 1

Translation: You sick puppy!

———————————— ❧ ————————————

Hug with swine!

King John V, 2

Translation: Go to your trough!

Would thou wert clean enough to spit upon!
Timon of Athens IV, 3

I'll beat thee, but I should infect my hands.
Timon of Athens IV, 3

Translation: You dirty rat!

Give me your hand. I can tell your fortune.
You are a fool.
The Two Noble Kinsmen III, 5

Translation: Cross my palm with silver. What a jerk!

CURSES AND
IMPRECATIONS

— ❦ —

*Used to bring every sort of disaster
on your enemy's head*

Boils and plagues
Plaster you o'er, that you may be abhorr'd
Farther than seen, and one infect another
Against the wind a mile.

Coriolanus I, 4

Translation: A plague on all your houses.

Make thy sepulchre,
And creep into it far before thy time.

Henry VI Part 3 : I, I

Translation: Go bury yourself.
or
Drop dead yesterday.

I would the milk
Thy mother gave thee when thou suck'dst her breast
Had been a little ratsbane for thy sake!

Henry VI Part 1: V, 4

Translation: I wish you'd never been born.

Be thou a prey.

Henry VI Part 3: I, 1

Translation: Fall victim.

Be thou the sullen presage of your own decay.

King John I, I

Translation: May you sense the foreboding
of you own demise.

or

May you be the dismal mirror of your own doom.

Eat my leek!

Henry V V, I

Translation: Bite the big one!

Laughest thou, wretch? Thy mirth shall turn to moan.

Henry VI Part I : II, 3

Translation: Laugh at your own risk.

I throw thy name against the bruising stones.

Two Gentlemen of Verona I, 2

Translation: Take that!

(This must be accompanied by action. In the play,
Julia tears her lover's name from a letter he has sent,
and throws the paper onto the ground.)

THE LONG GOOD-BYE

---

*Ways of saying "go away"
with as much offense as possible*

Thy back, I prithee.
Timon of Athens IV, 3

Translation: Turn tail.

Let's meet as little as we can.
As You Like It III, 2

Translation: I greatly value your absence.

I do desire we may be better strangers.

As You Like It III, 2

Translation: Not even lunch!

Mend my company, take away thyself.

Timon of Athens IV, 3

Translation: Do me a favor. Scram!

I do frown on thee with all my heart,
And if my eyes can wound, now let them kill thee.

As You Like It III, 5

Translation: What part of "No!" can't you understand?

Get thee to a nunnery.

Hamlet III, 1

Translation: Shove off, sister!